Janice VanCleave's
MOLECULES
Spectacular Science Projects

JANICE VANCLEAVE'S
SPECTACULAR SCIENCE PROJECTS

Animals
Gravity
Molecules

JANICE VANCLEAVE'S
SCIENCE FOR EVERY KID SERIES

Astronomy for Every Kid
Biology for Every Kid
Chemistry for Every Kid
Earth Science for Every Kid
Math for Every Kid
Physics for Every Kid

Janice VanCleave's
MOLECULES
Spectacular Science Projects

John Wiley & Sons, Inc.
New York · Chichester · Brisbane · Toronto · Singapore

In recognition of the importance of preserving what has been written, it is a policy of John Wiley & Sons, Inc. to have books of enduring value published in the United States printed on acid-free paper, and we exert our best efforts to that end.

Design and Production by BOOKMAKERS LTD.
Illustrated by KAREN PELLATON

Library of Congress Cataloging-in-Publication Data

VanCleave, Janice Pratt
    [Molecules]
      Janice VanCleave's molecules
            p.   cm. -- (Spectacular science projects)
      Includes index
      ISBN 0-471-55054-X

Printed in the United States of America
10 9 8 7

CONTENTS

Dedicated to My Daughter,
Whom I Love Very Much,

Ginger VanCleave Russell

Science is a search for answers. Science projects are good ways to learn more about science as you search for the answers to specific problems. This book will give you guidance and provide ideas, but you must do your part in the search by planning experiments, finding and recording information related to the problem, and organizing the data collected to find the answer to the problem. Sharing your findings by presenting your project at science fairs will be a rewarding experience if you have properly prepared the exhibit. Trying to assemble a project overnight results in frustration, and you cheat yourself out of the fun of being a science detective. Solving a scientific mystery, like solving a detective mystery, requires planning and the careful collecting of facts. The following sections provide suggestions for how to get started on this scientific quest. Start the project with curiosity and a desire to learn something new.

SELECT A TOPIC

The 20 topics in this book suggest many possible problems to solve. Each topic has one "cookbook" experiment—follow the recipe and the result is guaranteed. Approximate metric equivalents have been given after all English measurements. Try several or all of these easy experiments before choosing the topic you like best and want to know

more about. Regardless of the problem you choose to solve, what you discover will make you more knowledgeable about molecules.

KEEP A JOURNAL

Purchase a bound notebook in which you will write everything relating to the project. This is your journal. It will contain your original ideas as well as ideas you get from books or from people like teachers and scientists. It will include descriptions of your experiments as well as diagrams, photographs, and written observations of all your results. Every entry should be as neat as possible and dated. Information from this journal can be used to write a report of your project, and you will want to display the journal with your completed project. A neat, orderly journal provides a complete and accurate record of your project from start to finish. It is also proof of the time you spent sleuthing out the answers to the scientific mystery you undertook to solve.

LET'S EXPLORE

This section of each chapter follows each of the 20 sample experiments and provides additional questions about the problem presented in the experiment. By making small changes to some part of the sample experiment, new results are achieved. Think about why these new results might have happened.

SHOW TIME!

You can use the pattern of the sample experiment to design your own experiments to solve the questions asked in "Let's Explore." Your own experiment should follow the sample experiment's format and include a single question about one thing, a list of necessary materials, a detailed step-by-step procedure, written results with diagrams, graphs, and charts if they seem helpful, and a conclusion answering and explaining the question. Include any information you found through research to clarify your answer. When you design your own experiments, make sure to get adult approval if supplies or procedures other than those given in this book are used. If you want to make a science fair project, study the information listed here and after each sample experiment in the book to develop your ideas into a real science fair exhibit. Use the suggestions that best apply to the project topic that you have chosen. Keep in mind that while your display represents all the work that you have done, it must tell the story of the project in such a way that it attracts and holds the interest of the viewer. So keep it simple. Do not try to cram all your information into one place. To have more space on the display and still exhibit all your work, keep some of the charts, graphs, pictures, and other materials in your journal instead of on the display board itself.

The actual size and shape of displays can be different, depending on the local science fair officials, so you will have to check the rules for your science fair. Most exhibits are allowed to be 48 inches (122 cm) wide, 30 inches (76 cm) deep, and 108 inches (274 cm) high. These are maximum measurements and your display may be smaller than this. A three-sided backboard (see drawing) is usually the best way to display your work. Wooden panels can be hinged together, but you can also use sturdy cardboard pieces taped together to form a very inexpensive but presentable exhibit.

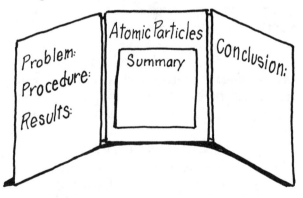

A good title of six words or less with a maximum of 50 characters should be placed at the top of the center panel. The title should capture the theme of the project but should not be the same as the problem statement. For example, if the problem under question is "What are atoms composed of?" a good title for the project might be "Atomic Particles." The title and other headings should be neat and large enough to be readable at a distance of about 3 feet (1 meter). You can glue letters to the backboard (you can use precut letters that you buy or letters that you cut out of construction paper), or you can stencil the letters for all the titles. A short summary paragraph of about 100 words to explain the scientific principles involved is good and can be printed under the title. A person who has no knowledge of the topic should be able to easily understand the basic idea of the project just from reading the summary.

There are no set rules about the position of the information on the display. However, it all needs to be well organized, with the title and summary paragraph as the main point at the top of the center panel and the remaining material placed neatly from left to right under specific headings. Choices of headings will depend on how you wish to display the information. Separate headings for Problem, Procedure, Results, and Conclusion may be used.

The judges give points for how clearly you are able to discuss the project and explain its purpose, procedure, results and conclusion. The display should be organized so that it explains everything, but your ability to discuss your project and answer the questions of the judges convinces them that you did the work and understand what you have done. Practice a speech in front of friends, and invite them to ask you questions. If you do not know the answer to a question, never guess or make up an answer or just say, "I do not know." Instead, you can say that you did not discover that answer during your research and then offer other information that you found of interest about the project. Be proud of the project and approach the judges with enthusiasm about your work.

CHECK IT OUT!

Read about your topic in many books and magazines. You are more likely to have a successful project if you are well informed about the topic. For the topics in this book, some tips are provided about specific places to look for information. Record in your journal all the information you find, and include for each source the author's name, the name of the book, the numbers of the pages you read, the publisher's name, where it was published, and the year of publication.

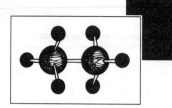

BUILDING BLOCKS

How can you make a model of a lithium atom?

MATERIALS

scissors
ruler
stiff wire
modeling clay, red, green,
    and yellow
string

PROCEDURE

1. Cut two lengths of wire, one 12 inches (30 cm) long and the other 18 inches (45 cm) long.

2. Twist the ends of the wires together.

Then bend and shape the wires into two circles, one within the other.

3. Press the ends of the twisted wires into a lump of clay so that the circles are standing up.

4. Cut a 6-inch (15 cm) length of string.

5. Tie the string to the top of the inner wire circle so that the free end of the string hangs in the center of the circle.

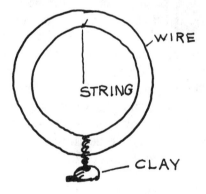

6. Mold small balls (about as big as the tip of your little finger) from the three colors of clay. Make three balls of red clay, three yellow, and four green.

7. Press two of the red balls onto the inner circle of wire, one on each side.

8. Press the third ball of red clay onto the outer circle of wire, on the right side.

9. Press the yellow clay balls and green clay balls together around the string so that they are hanging at the center of the circle.

10. Trim away any excess string.

11. Make a key for the lithium structure as in the diagram.

RESULTS

You have made a three-dimensional model of a lithium atom, showing the position of the atom's electrons (red), protons (yellow), and neutrons (green).

WHY?

Atoms are the smallest building blocks of **matter** (a substance that takes up space and has weight). The combination of two or more atoms produces **molecules.**

Atoms themselves are made of even smaller particles that have electrical properties. These particles are **protons** (which have a positive charge), **electrons** (which have a negative charge), and **neutrons** (which are neutral, having neither a positive nor a negative charge). A lithium atom has three protons and four neutrons in its **nucleus** (the central part of the atom) and three electrons outside the nucleus. Notice that the number of electrons and protons is the same; this is true in all atoms. The electrons move within an area around the nucleus called an **electron shell,** which is represented by each wire loop in your model.

LET'S EXPLORE

1. In 1910, Frederick Soddy of England discovered that atoms of the same **element** (substance in its simplest form) can differ in mass. He determined that the difference in mass is due to the presence of different numbers of neutrons in their nuclei. Atoms of the same element, but with different masses, are called **isotopes.** Construct an isotope of lithium by repeating the activity. Add an additional neutron by using five balls of green clay to represent five neutrons. **Science Fair Hint:** Display the model as part of a project.

2. An atom is identified by the number of protons in its nucleus. Changing the number of protons changes the **chemical properties** (the way the atom behaves) of the atom. Repeat the activity, and use the "Atomic Particles" chart for information about the number of atomic particles in the

ten different atoms. Note that some of the atoms have electrons in two electron shells. For these atoms, two wire loops, as in the lithium model, are needed. For atoms with electrons in one energy shell, use the helium model as an example. **Science Fair Hint:** Construct the ten models, and use them as part of a project display.

SHOW TIME

Hydrogen has three different isotopes, H-1, H-2, and H-3. Use the "Hydrogen Isotopes" chart to construct and display models of the three hydrogen isotopes. A report about the uses of these isotopes can be included with the display.

ATOMIC PARTICLES

Name	Symbol	Particles in the Nucleus		Electrons in Electron Shell	
		Protons	Neutrons	#1	#2
Hydrogen	H	1	0	1	0
Helium	He	2	2	2	0
Lithium	Li	3	4	2	1
Beryllium	Be	4	5	2	2
Boron	B	5	6	2	3
Carbon	C	6	6	2	4
Nitrogen	N	7	7	2	5
Oxygen	O	8	8	2	6
Fluorine	F	9	10	2	7
Neon	Ne	10	10	2	8

HYDROGEN ISOTOPES

Name	Symbol	Particles in the Nucleus		Electrons in First Electron Shell
		Protons	Neutrons	
Hydrogen-1	H-1	1	0	1
Hydrogen-2	H-2	1	1	1
Hydrogen-3	H-3	1	2	1

CHECK IT OUT!

There are more than 100 different kinds of atoms. Dmitri Mendeleev, a Russian chemist, designed a chart commonly called the *Periodic Chart*. About 45 years after Mendeleev's chart was constructed, Moseley, an English scientist, changed the chart. Read about the Periodic Chart, and write a report about the charts of these two scientists. Include information on how the charts are similar and how they differ. Display a current Periodic Chart with your report.

SUPER CHAINS

PROBLEM

What is the physical structure of methane, the simplest **hydrocarbon** *(molecules containing hydrogen and carbon atoms)?*

• MATERIALS
4 toothpicks
1 large black gumdrop
4 small white gumdrops

PROCEDURE

1. Stick 4 toothpicks in 1 large black gumdrop. Space the toothpicks so that they are an equal distance from each other.

2. Place 1 small white gumdrop on the end of each toothpick.

RESULTS

You have made a molecular model for methane.

WHY?

Hydrocarbon molecules are composed of carbon and hydrogen atoms. Each carbon atom in a hydrocarbon molecule has four **bonds** (connections between atoms) that are equally spaced, and each hydrogen atom has one bond. Methane is the simplest hydrocarbon molecule. In the methane structure, the single black gumdrop represents one carbon atom bonded (attached) to four hydrogen atoms represented by the white gumdrops. The chemical formula used to represent methane is CH_4. The formula, like the model you made, shows that the methane

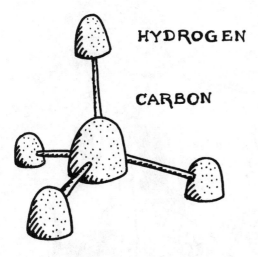

HYDROGEN

CARBON

METHANE

model, first connect two large black gumdrops with a toothpick. Then stick three toothpicks in each of the connected black gumdrops. Space the toothpicks so that all the toothpicks in each black gumdrop are an equal distance from each other. Place one small white gumdrop on the end of each toothpick. **Science Fair Hint:** Display models of methane and ethane as part of a project.

molecule has one carbon atom and four hydrogen atoms.

LET'S EXPLORE

What would be the shape of a hydrocarbon with two carbon atoms? Ethane contains two carbon atoms and six hydrogen atoms. The chemical formula for ethane is C_2H_6. To construct an ethane

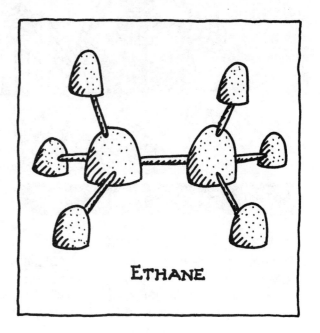

ETHANE

SHOW TIME!

1. What shapes do other hydrocarbons such as propane (C_3H_8) and butane (C_4H_{10}) have? Remember that each carbon atom in a hydrocarbon molecule has four bonds that are equally spaced, and each hydrogen atom has one bond. Display all the models constructed as part of a project display.

2. A structural formula for a hydrocarbon molecule is used to illustrate the number of connected carbon and hydrogen atoms. Complete the "Hydrocarbons" chart and display with the models of each molecule.

HYDROCARBONS

NAME	FORMULA	STRUCTURAL FORMULA
Methane	CH_4	$\begin{array}{c} \text{H} \\ | \\ \text{H}-\text{C}-\text{H} \\ | \\ \text{H} \end{array}$
Ethane	C_2H_6	$\begin{array}{c} \text{H} \quad \text{H} \\ | \quad\; | \\ \text{H}-\text{C}-\text{C}-\text{H} \\ | \quad\; | \\ \text{H} \quad \text{H} \end{array}$
Propane	C_3H_8	
Butane	C_4H_{10}	

CHECK IT OUT!

Read about hydrocarbon gases such as methane, ethane, propane, and butane. Write and display a report about these gases. Include in the report answers to questions such as:

- Why is methane called marsh gas?
- Which of the gases are used as home fuels?

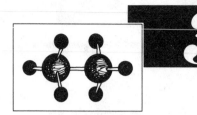

BREAKDOWN

PROBLEM

What happens when the shape of a protein molecule is changed?

MATERIALS
raw egg
2-quart (2 liter) bowl
fork

PROCEDURE

1. Ask an adult to help you separate the yolk from the white portion of the egg, placing the egg white in a bowl and discarding the yolk and eggshell.

2. Allow the egg white to sit undisturbed at room temperature for 20 minutes.

3. Dip the fork into the egg white, and lift the fork above the bowl.

4. Observe the texture and color of the egg white on the fork.

5. Return the egg white to the bowl.

6. With a quick whipping motion, use the fork to beat the egg white.

7. After about 50 strokes, lift the egg white again and observe its texture and color.

8. Continue to whip the egg white about two minutes or until no further change in appearance is observed.

RESULTS

Before beating, the egg white actually has a pale yellow color and a slimy texture. It slowly flows off the fork and back into the bowl. After beating, the color is white, and the texture is soft and foamy. The foamy egg white takes up more space than the slimy egg white.

WHY?

Denaturing means to change something from its natural form. The egg white's natural form looks like a pale yellow, slimy liquid. In its natural form, the egg white contains about 85 percent water and about 10 percent protein. It is the protein that is being denatured by the whipping action. Protein molecules are essential to all living animal cells for the growth and repair of tissue. These molecules are similar to balls of yarn, and beating the egg white causes the balls of proteins to unravel. The shape of this new unwound protein molecule traps air and thus forms a foam that can be three times the original size of the molecule. Colors of molecules change as the molecules rearrange themselves.

LET'S EXPLORE

1. Does the temperature of the egg affect the size of the resulting whipped egg whites? Chill water in a bowl by putting ice in it. Put warm water from a faucet in another bowl. In a third bowl put cold water from a faucet. Put an egg in each container of water, and leave them for at least 10 minutes. Then separate and beat the egg whites. Display photographs or

drawings of the eggs in the containers of water. Observe and record the results. **Science Fair Hint:** Photographs or drawings of the resulting egg whites along with a description of the results can be used as part of a project display.

2. When making meringue (whipped egg whites), cooks add about ⅛ teaspoon (0.6 ml) of cream of tartar to make the foam last longer. Does the cream of tartar actually make the foam last longer? Test this by beating the whites from two eggs separately. Add about ⅛ teaspoon (0.6 ml) of cream of tartar to one egg white before beating it, and leave the other one plain. Let the two bowls stand for 30 minutes, and observe and record any differences in the foam of the egg whites. **Science Fair Hint:** Photographs taken of the bowls before and after standing can be displayed as part of a project display.

SHOW TIME!

1. Can proteins be denatured in ways other than beating? Acids denature some proteins. You can use vinegar (an acid) to demonstrate the effect of acids on the protein in milk. Add 1 tablespoon (15 ml) of vinegar to 1 cup (250 ml) of milk. Observe and record any change in the appearance of the milk. Use results as part of a written report about the project.

2. As part of a project display, use two equally small, fist-size balls of yarn to represent protein molecules. One of the balls can be labeled "Protein." Unwind the second ball of yarn, and separate the individual strands of fiber. Label this fluffy mass "Denatured Protein."

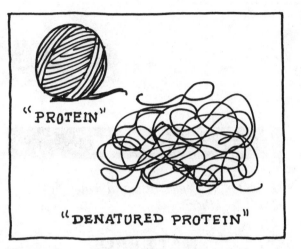

"PROTEIN"

"DENATURED PROTEIN"

CHECK IT OUT!

Coagulation (the forming of a thickened solid mass) is another kind of denaturing. As part of the project report, include information about coagulation such as:
- What happens when a protein coagulates?
- Why do some foods that contain protein, such as meats, eggs, and batters, become firm when cooked?

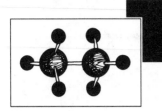

4

PROBLEM

Do water molecules in liquid water fit tightly together?

MATERIALS

clear drinking glass
plate
pitcher of water
paper towel
1 teaspoon (5 ml) measuring
 spoon
salt

PROCEDURE

1. Place the glass on the plate.

2. Fill the glass to the brim with water. Stop adding the water when a tiny stream of water starts to flow over the side of the glass. (If you look sideways at the surface of the water, you can see it "bulging" over the top of the glass.)

3. Without moving the glass or plate, carefully blot up the water in the plate with a paper towel.

4. Fill the measuring spoon with salt.

5. Very slowly sprinkle salt crystals into the glass of water. If you use the entire spoonful, fill the spoon again.

6. Continue to add salt until water spills over the top of the glass. Keep track of how much salt you use.

7. Record the amount of salt required to cause the water to spill.

RESULTS

Two to three teaspoons of salt can be added before the water spills.

WHY?

The grains of salt are made of tiny molecules. These molecules break away from each other and freely move around in the water. The water molecules in liquid water are connected in such a way that small empty pockets are formed. Separate salt molecules are small enough to easily fit into the spaces between the connected water molecules, so they do not take up any extra space.

1. Would other crystals give the same results? Repeat the experiment using granular sugar, powdered sugar, and/or sand. Measure and record the amount of material added to the water before it spills.

2. Would the temperature of the water affect the results? Repeat the experiment using warm water from the faucet, and then repeat using icy water.

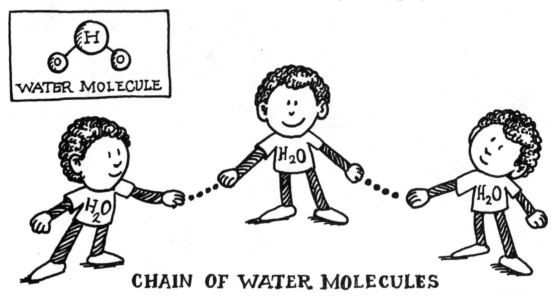

WATER MOLECULE

CHAIN OF WATER MOLECULES

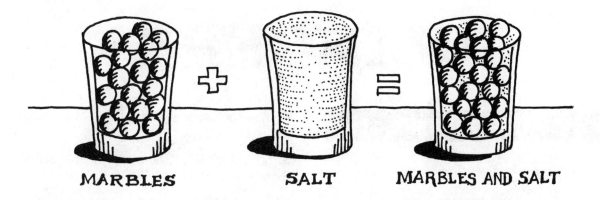

MARBLES   SALT   MARBLES AND SALT

SHOW TIME!

1. Would a liquid fit into the spaces in the connected water molecules? Mix 1 cup (250 ml) of rubbing alcohol and 1 cup (250 ml) of water together in a large measuring cup. Observe and record the resulting volume. *(Note: Do not get the alcohol near your eyes or mouth.)*

2. Display models to explain the spacing between molecules. Fill a glass with marbles and measure the amount of salt that can be poured into the glass of marbles.

CHECK IT OUT!

1. What is the shape of water molecules? What do they look like in liquid water? One reference source is an experiment called "Where Did It Go?," page 26 in Janice VanCleave's *Chemistry for Every Kid,* (New York: Wiley, 1989).

2. How large are molecules? Salt molecules are so tiny that it would take 25 million molecules laid end to end to span 1 inch (10 million for 1 cm). Find out the size of other molecules used in your experiments.

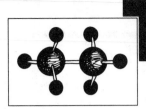

CLINGERS

PROBLEM

Why can water flow at an angle?

MATERIALS

scissors
ruler
cotton kite string
1 cup (250 ml) measuring
   cup with handle
water
drinking glass
cookie sheet

PROCEDURE

1. Cut an 18-inch (45 cm) length of string.

2. Tie one end of the string around the top of the measuring cup's handle.

3. Fill the cup with water.

4. Wet the entire length of the string with water.

5. Set the glass in the center of the cookie sheet.

6. Lay the string over the spout of the measuring cup.

7. Hold the free end of the string against the inside of the glass.

8. Separate the cup and glass so the string is tight.

9. Raise the bottom of the cup about 12 inches (30 cm) from the cookie sheet.

10. Slowly pour the water out of the cup.

RESULTS

The water flows down the string into the glass.

WHY?

Water molecules attract each other. This force of attraction between like molecules is called **cohesion.** Under the surface of the liquid, each molecule is attracted by other molecules that pull on each other in all directions. At the surface of the liquid, the molecules are only pulled to the sides

and downward. This unbalanced force tends to draw the water molecules at the surface closer together, forming a tough, elastic, skinlike film across the water. This tendency of water molecules to cling together at the surface is called **surface tension.** The water in the wet string attracts the molecules in the falling water. The surface tension on the outside of the flowing water holds the water close to the string as it flows down the slanted string.

1. Would the height of the measuring cup affect the results? Repeat the experiment, changing the height of the cup. Keep a record of the various heights and their results by standing a yardstick (meterstick) behind the cup. **Science Fair Hint:** Have a helper take photographs as you test the results at different heights. Use these photographs with a written report of the

results as part of a project display.

2. Would the length of the string affect the results? Repeat the experiment, but change the string's length. Test with shorter and longer lengths of string. Observe and record any difference in the flow of the water.

3. Would the results be the same if a different type of string was used? Repeat the experiment using strings made of different materials.

4. How important is it to wet the string? Repeat the original experiment using a dry string.

occurrences such as:

- insects walking across the surface of water
- raindrops taking the shape of a sphere
- water flowing out of a tap and forming a smooth tube

SHOW TIME!

1. How close do molecules of water have to be to attract? Place drops of water on a piece of wax paper. Use a toothpick to slowly push a drop of water close to a second drop. Record the distance at which an attraction between the drops is observed.

2. Find and display examples of how surface tension accounts for common

CHECK IT OUT!

If an astronaut squeezed the bulb of an eyedropper containing liquid in a near zero-gravity environment, the falling drops of liquid would be in the shape of a sphere. Find out how surface tension affects the shapes of the liquid drops. Diagrams showing the forces on the liquid molecules can be displayed.

ON THE MOVE

6

PROBLEM

Are water molecules in constant motion?

MATERIALS

1-cup (250 ml) measuring
   cup
water
¼ teaspoon (1 ml) salt
spoon
green food coloring
clear drinking glass, about 8
   ounces (250 ml)
index card

PROCEDURE

1. Measure ¼ cup (60 ml) water into the measuring cup.

2. Add the salt to the water, and stir until the salt is dissolved.

3. Stir drops of green food coloring into the salty water until it is a dark green color.

4. Fill the drinking glass one-fourth full with plain water.

5. Tilt the glass to the side, and slowly pour the green salt water down the side.

6. Cover the top of the glass with an index card to protect the contents.

WATER
GREEN SALTY WATER

7. Place the glass where it will not be disturbed for two days.

8. Observe the glass as often as possible during the two days. Record the time and the results of each observation.

RESULTS

The green salty water settles to the bottom of the glass and the clear water floats on top with a definite division between the two layers. After about one hour, a pale green layer appears just above the darker green layer of salty water. This band

continues to widen as time passes. After 48 hours, all of the liquid in the glass is one color, green.

WHY?

The green salty water floats under the clear water because the salt water is heavier than the clear water. With time, the definite boundary between the two layers of liquid becomes less distinct because the liquids mix together. This mixing is caused by the constant motion of the water molecules in the liquids. Some of the pure water moves into the green salty water, and some of the salty water moves into the pure water. When the glass stands undisturbed long enough, the two liquids become completely mixed. The mixing of molecules because of molecular motion is called **diffusion.**

LET'S EXPLORE

1. Does the amount of salt affect the **rate of diffusion,** the speed at which the liquids mix? Repeat the experiment using different measures of salt. Label the separate containers. Observe, and record the time and the results of each observation. **Science Fair Hint:** Use photographs and/or diagrams to aid in describing the results.

2. Are water molecules moving from the upper clear water layer downward? To demonstrate the fact that water molecules from the upper and lower layers are moving around, color each layer with a different color. **Science Fair Hint:** Colored diagrams could be used to represent the results at different time periods, and these diagrams can be part of a project display.

SHOW TIME!

1. Do gas molecules diffuse? Open a bottle of perfume. Set it in the corner of a room. Record the time required for the scent to reach various distances from the bottle. Evenly space four helpers in front of the open perfume bottle. The first helper should hold the bottle in his/her hands. Have the helpers raise one hand as soon as they smell the perfume. Take pictures of the group as each hand is raised. Display

the pictures and the times taken.

2. What is **diffusion?** Give more than a definition of the term. Observe and discover common examples of diffusion in the world around you such as:

- You know what is being cooked in the kitchen when you enter the front door of your home.
- You can smell someone's perfume in a room even after they've left the room.
- Solid sticks of fertilizer are placed in the ground near the stem of plants.

Pictures and diagrams representing these and other examples of diffusion make a good project display.

CHECK IT OUT!

Does diffusion occur in solids? Will the molecules of two solids placed in close contact together diffuse? If there is diffusion between solids, how does the rate of diffusion of solids compare to that of liquids and gases? Include the answers to the questions as well as other facts on diffusion in the project report.

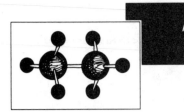

7

UPHILL CLIMBERS

PROBLEM

Why does water rise in a paper towel?

MATERIALS

scissors
ruler
paper towel
red food coloring
cellophane tape
pencil
water
glass jar about 6 inches (15
   cm) tall

PROCEDURE

1. Cut a 2 × 8-inch (5 × 20 cm) strip from the paper towel.

2. Place a drop of red food coloring 2 inches (5 cm) from one end of the paper strip.

3. Tape the uncolored end of the paper to the center of the pencil. Roll some of the paper around the pencil.

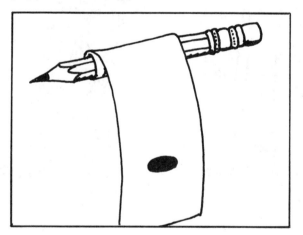

4. Pour 1 inch (2.5 cm) of water into the jar.

5. Lower the paper into the jar. Unroll the paper-towel strip until the bottom edge just touches the water.

RESULTS

The water dissolves the red coloring as it rises in the paper strip. The red coloring spreads outward and upward.

WHY?

The paper is made of tiny fibers. The spacing of the fibers forms tube-like structures throughout the paper. The water can be seen zigzagging through these spaces. Adhesive and cohesive forces help to pull the water upward. **Adhesion** is the attraction that each water molecule has for the paper. **Cohesion** is the attraction that water molecules have for each other. The water's surface within the spaces is not flat but slightly crescent-shaped. This is because the adhesion of water to the paper is greater than the cohesion between the water molecules. The adhesive attraction of water to the paper is strong enough to move the water up the sides of the fiber tubes against the downward pull of gravity. The water molecules clinging to the fiber then pull the lower water molecules up the center of the tube. The movement of the water up through the tiny tubes is called **capillary action.**

LET'S EXPLORE

1. Does the color of the dye on the paper affect the results? Use different colors of

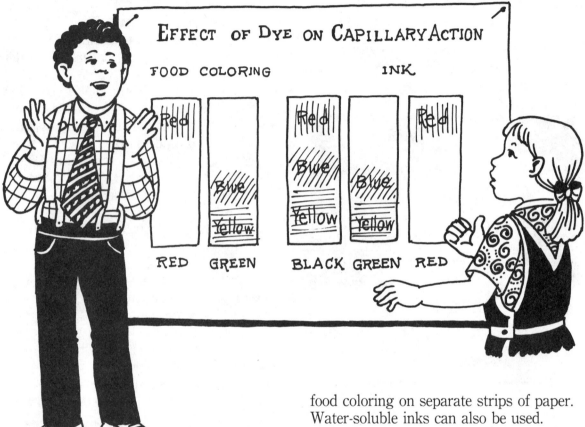

food coloring on separate strips of paper. Water-soluble inks can also be used.
Science Fair Hint: Dry all of the strips and, with a summary of the results, use as part of a project display such as the one shown.

2. Does the type of paper used affect the capillary action of the water? Use a variety of paper samples, for example, coffee filters, paper sacks, and facial tissue. Different brands of paper towels could be tested for their absorbing abilities.

SHOW TIME!

1. Does water rise better in small or large spaces? Secure two flat pieces of glass

(MATCH SEPARATES GLASS)

together so that the space between them changes. The illustration shows one method of preparing the materials to explore the answer to this question. Colored water makes it easier to view the height of the liquid between the glass plates. The materials can be used as a project display along with a diagram and summary of the results.

2. Make a list of some common and important applications of capillary action in daily life. Some examples are:
- the absorbent action of blotters and towels
- liquid rising in the wicks of lanterns and candles
- the surfacing of water through tiny cracks in the soil

CHECK IT OUT!

A project report could include information about the movement of liquids up the stems of plants due to capillary action. Is there a limit to the height that water can be raised due to capillary action?

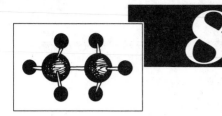

TUG OF WAR

8

PROBLEM

Why do some materials get wetter than others?

MATERIALS
drinking glass
liquid cooking oil
eyedropper
water

PROCEDURE

1. Turn the drinking glass upside down on a table.

2. Rub a drop of oil on one half of the bottom surface of the glass.

3. Fill the eyedropper with water.

4. Hold the end of the dropper about 2 inches (5 cm) above the unoiled, upturned bottom of the glass.

5. Allow only one drop of water to fall onto the glass.

6. Observe and record the shape of the water drop. Make a drawing as part of the description of the drop's shape.

7. Squeeze one drop of water from the eyedropper onto the oiled surface.

8. Observe and record the shape of the water drop.

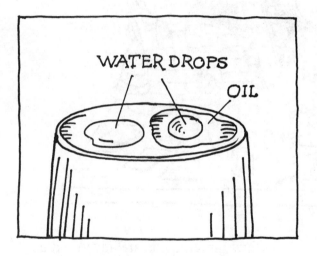

WATER DROPS

OIL

RESULTS

The water drop spreads out and flattens on the clean surface of the glass. The drop of water on the oiled surface is more spherical, ball-like, in shape.

WHY?

The shape of the water drops is due to two different forces, cohesion and adhesion. **Cohesion** is the force of attraction between the water molecules. The water molecules pull on each other, and this cohesive force gives the drops of liquid a spherical or ball-like shape. **Adhesion** is the force of attraction between different molecules. Glass strongly attracts the water molecules, and it is this adhesive force that causes the water drop to flatten and spread out. Water is said to "wet" a surface if it spreads out on the material. The more the water spreads out, the more the water wets the surface. The wetting ability of water depends on the adhesive force between the surface molecules and the water molecules. The adhesion between an oily surface and water molecules is very small, and thus a drop of water on an oily surface retains its somewhat spherical shape.

LET'S EXPLORE

1. Do liquid laundry detergents increase the wetting ability of water? Add varying

amounts of laundry detergent to the water in the eyedropper, and repeat the experiment. Try different brands of laundry detergent, and compare their wetting abilities. **Science Fair Hint:** Results of this comparison can be used as part of a display.

2. Dishwashing liquids are advertised as having the ability to clean dishes without leaving spots. Find out what they do to the water that could produce this "no spotting" result. Repeat the experiment adding dishwashing liquid to the water in the eyedropper.

SHOW TIME!

What materials does water "wet" the best? Squeeze water drops onto different materials such as aluminum foil, paper towels, cloth, wax paper, writing paper, newspaper, and other available samples. Keep small samples of each test material to accompany the summary report as part of a project display. Diagrams of the shapes of the water drops on each material should be part of the description given in the summary report.

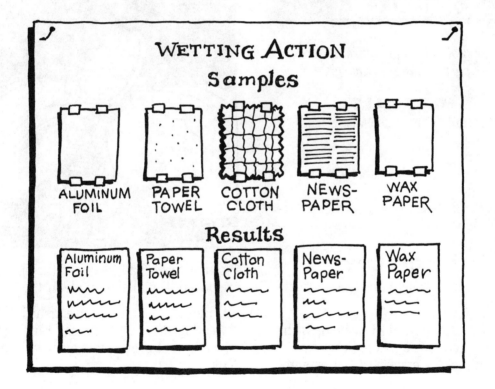

ESCAPE

Can water molecules move through the membrane surrounding a raw egg?

MATERIALS

2 1-cup (250 ml) measuring
   cups
water
2 raw eggs in their shells
metal spoon
masking tape
marking pen

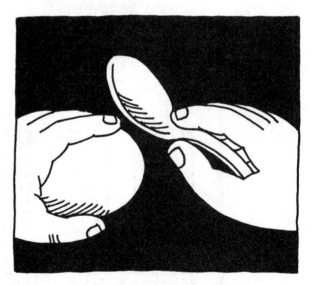

PROCEDURE

1. Fill each measuring cup three-fourths full with water.

2. Tap the rounded end of one egg with the bowl of the metal spoon. Be very gentle and make a crack just big enough so that two small pieces of the shell can be removed to make one hole in the shell.

3. Remove the pieces of eggshell without breaking the thin egg membrane. If the membrane breaks, start over with another egg.

thin-skinned bubble has pushed out through one of the cracks (after a while the bubble breaks). There is no visible change in the shell of the uncracked egg in cup #2.

4. Carefully place the egg with the cracked shell in a cup of water.

5. Use the masking tape and marking pen to label this cup #1.

6. Place the unbroken egg in the remaining cup of water. This egg must not be cracked.

7. Label this cup #2.

8. Allow the cups to stand undisturbed two to three days.

9. Observe and record the appearance of each egg.

RESULTS
The egg with the missing pieces of eggshell has large cracks, and a

WHY?
The water molecules moved through the thin membrane surrounding the egg by a process called osmosis. Two critical factors affecting the movement of water by osmosis are (1) the amount of water and dissolved material inside the membrane, and (2) the amount of water and dissolved material outside the membrane. **Osmosis** is the movement of molecules, such as water, through a membrane. The water always moves toward the side containing the most dissolved material and the lesser amount of water. In this experiment, the dissolved material is the content of the egg. The water in the cup moves inside the egg, causing the egg membrane to swell, push the cracks apart as part of the swollen egg pushes through the crack, and finally break. The unbroken egg remains unchanged because the water does not penetrate the hard eggshell.

LET'S EXPLORE

1. Would the size of the shell pieces removed affect the results?

a) Repeat the experiment using eggs with different sized pieces removed from the shell. Make diagrams to illustrate the size of the membrane exposed.

b) The entire shell of the egg can be removed without breaking the membrane by soaking the egg in white vinegar for 48 hours. Measure the egg before it is placed in the vinegar and again after 48 hours. Determine if the entire vinegar solution moves through the membrane or only the water molecules in the vinegar.

2. Can materials dissolved in water move through the membrane of the egg? Repeat the experiment using an egg with tiny shell pieces missing, but place the egg in a cup of water containing 10 drops of green food coloring. Break the egg after 24 hours and observe the color of the contents.

SHOW TIME!

Will water molecules move through other cell membranes? Place different slices of food in bowls of water and test their firmness before and after soaking in the water. Potato and cucumber slices change in about 30 minutes. In 24 hours, raisins show a dramatic result that can be displayed. Diagrams, along with a description of the results for each food, can be displayed.

CHECK IT OUT!

What is the role of osmosis in digestion? An experiment called "Small Intestine," page 200 in *Biology for Every Kid* (New York: Wiley, 1990), by Janice VanCleave, can be used to discover how soluble materials move through the lining of the small intestine of animals.

MIXERS

PROBLEM

Can the addition of sugar to water form a **homogeneous mixture** *(a mixture that is the same throughout)?*

MATERIALS

spoon
drinking glass
dishwashing liquid
water
paper towel
distilled water
1 teaspoon (5 ml) sugar
drinking straw

PROCEDURE

Note: Never taste anything in a laboratory setting unless you are sure that there are no harmful chemicals or materials and that all containers are properly cleaned. This experiment is safe since only sugar and water are present.

1. Prepare the materials by washing the spoon and glass in soapy water.

2. Rinse the spoon and glass in clear water, and dry them with the paper towel.

3. Fill the cleaned glass half full with distilled water.

4. Add the sugar to the distilled water.

5. Stir until no sugar particles can be seen.

6. Stand a clean straw in the glass containing the sugar-water mixture.

7. Hold your finger on the top of the straw as you raise the straw out of the glass. (The sugar-water mixture stays in the straw.)

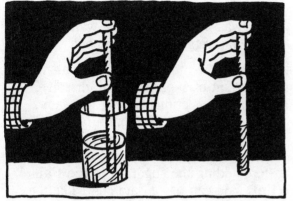

solute (sugar) dissolves in the **solvent** (water). The molecules in the crystals of sugar separate and move between the molecules of water. The sugar-water solution is **homogeneous,** meaning the solution is the same throughout. Samples of equal volumes taken from the solution would contain the same number of sugar molecules and water molecules regardless of where the samples were taken.

8. Taste the liquid, and make a mental note of its sweetness.

9. Use the straw to taste samples from the bottom, middle, and top of the sugar-water mixture.

10. Compare the taste of the three samples.

RESULTS

All three samples have the same sweet taste.

WHY?

Sugar and water form a special mixture called a solution. **Solutions** are produced by combining a solute with a solvent. The

LET'S EXPLORE

1. How much sugar will dissolve in water? Use 1 cup (250 ml) of distilled water. Add 1 teaspoon (5 ml) of sugar at a time, stirring after each addition until all the sugar dissolves. Continue to add and record measured amounts of sugar to the water until the particles stop dissolving no matter how much you stir. A solution that will not dissolve any more solute is said to be **saturated.**

2. Would the amount of sugar needed to make a saturated solution change if the water was not distilled? Use water from a faucet and repeat the experiment.

3. Does the temperature of the water affect the amount of sugar that will dissolve? Repeat the experiment using ice water, cold, and warm water from a faucet. Place a thermometer in the water and record the temperature. Remove the thermometer before adding the sugar. **Science Fair Hint:** You can use a data chart like the one below to record and display the temperature of each liquid and the amount of sugar needed to produce a saturated solution.

DATA CHART
TEMPERATURE VS AMOUNT OF SOLUTE

Temperature		Amount of Solute (Sugar)
Cold . . . . _____°F . . . (_____°C)		_____tsp . . . (_____ml)
Moderate . . . . _____°F . . . (_____°C)		_____tsp . . . (_____ml)
Warm . . . . _____°F . . . (_____°C)		_____tsp . . . (_____ml)

SHOW TIME!

1. Find out the meaning of the following terms:

- solute
- solvent
- solution
- dilute
- concentrated
- saturated
- unsaturated

The solutions diagram provides an example of how the terms might be displayed.

2. Solutions are mixtures in which a substance is dissolved in another substance. The sugar-water solution is an example of a solid dissolved in a liquid. Learn about and display other types of solutions such as:

- a gas dissolved in a liquid (soda)
- a gas dissolved in a gas (air)
- a liquid dissolved in a gas (water in air)

CHECK IT OUT!

A solid dissolved in a solid is called an **alloy.** When metals are mixed together,

SOLUTIONS

WATER (SOLVENT)

SUGAR (SOLUTE)

WATER + SUGAR (SOLUTION)

DILUTE

CONCENTRATED

their properties change. Brass is an alloy of zinc and copper. It is harder and lasts longer than either zinc or copper alone. Alloys are used instead of pure metal because of their special properties. Find out more about alloys such as brass, bronze, pewter, and alnico. What are their special properties, and how are they used?

SEPARATE

Does the size of drops in an **emulsion**
*(two liquids that do not mix) affect the rate
at which the two liquids separate?*

MATERIALS

1 cup (250 ml) vegetable oil
1 quart (1 liter) jar with lid
1 cup (250 ml) white vinegar
green food coloring
timer

PROCEDURE

1. Pour the oil into the jar.

2. To the vinegar, add one drop of green
food coloring.

3. Pour the colored vinegar into the jar
containing the oil.

4. Observe the position of the two liquids
in the jar.

5. Close the lid on the jar.

6. Shake the jar vigorously five times, and then allow it to stand undisturbed.

7. Observe the contents of the jar as it stands. Look for drops of oil in the vinegar and drops of vinegar in the oil.

8. Use the timer to record the length of time needed for the two liquids to form two separate layers.

RESULTS

Green and colorless droplets are seen throughout the mixture. The time for separation depends on how hard the jar is shaken; the more vigorously the jar is shaken, the longer the separation time.

WHY?

The oil and colored vinegar are immiscible liquids. **Immiscible** means the liquids do not mix but form two separate layers with the lighter liquid (oil) floating on top of the heavier liquid (vinegar). A combination of two immiscible liquids is called an **emulsion.** Shaking an emulsion causes droplets of one liquid to float around in the other liquid. Shaking an oil-vinegar emulsion results in vinegar droplets in the oil layer and oil droplets in the vinegar layer. Each drop of oil contains many molecules of oil held together by cohesion. **Cohesion** is a force of attraction between like molecules. The vinegar drops contain molecules of vinegar and green food coloring all bound together by cohesion. This force of attraction between like molecules causes the drops to pull together and form separate layers. The smaller the droplets, the longer it takes for them to collect together and separate into layers. The green coloring and oil are immiscible, whereas the coloring and the vinegar are **miscible** (they mix in each other). This results in only the vinegar being colored.

LET'S EXPLORE

How can the liquids be separated for extended periods of time? Something called an **emulsifying agent** can be added to prevent the oil droplets from coming together. Try adding a raw egg to the jar containing the vinegar and oil. Shake vigorously about 40 times. Allow the jar to stand undisturbed. Record the length of time for any separation to be observed.

SHOW TIME!

1. With adult supervision, you can make a common **colloid,** an emulsion that does not separate. The egg acts as an **emulsifier** (something that helps liquids emulsify). Record the changes in the appearance of the mixture as each ingredient is added. Photographs can be taken to illustrate the descriptions. (*Note: Never taste anything in a laboratory setting unless you are sure that there are no harmful chemicals or materials, and that all containers are properly cleaned.*)

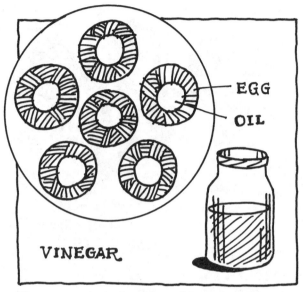

EGG

OIL

VINEGAR

The mayonnaise produced here is safe to eat if instructions are followed exactly and care is taken to use clean containers. Use the following recipe.

Homemade Mayonnaise
INGREDIENTS

1 egg yolk
bowl
1 tablespoon (15 ml) vinegar
¾ cup (188 ml) vegetable oil
eyedropper
eggbeater
lemon

spoon
1-pint (500 ml) jar with lid
refrigerator

DIRECTIONS

1. Place the egg yolk in the bowl, and slowly add 1 tablespoon (15 ml) of vinegar to the egg yolk.
2. Add 5 drops of oil with the eyedropper.
3. Beat the mixture thoroughly.
4. Add 5 more drops of oil and beat thoroughly.
5. Add the remaining oil 1 teaspoon (5 ml) at a time, beating thoroughly each time.
6. Season to taste with juice from the lemon.
7. Transfer to a jar with a spoon. Cover and store in the refrigerator.

2. How does an emulsifier work? Find out and explain how an emulsifier such as an egg keeps droplets of oil evenly spread throughout vinegar in a common colloid called mayonnaise.

3. Homogenized milk is a colloid. This means the fat droplets are evenly spread throughout the liquid and do not separate on standing. How is milk homogenized?

CRYSTALS

12

PROBLEM

What causes the shape of Epsom salt crystals that form when the solvent (water) evaporates from the salt solution?

MATERIALS

dishwashing liquid with
   squeeze top
clear, transparent, plastic
   folder
small paintbrush
1 tablespoon (15 ml) Epsom
   salts
clear drinking glass
1-tablespoon (15 ml)
   measuring spoon
water
spoon

PROCEDURE

1. Squeeze 3 drops of dishwashing liquid onto the center of the plastic folder.

2. Use a paintbrush to evenly spread the dishwashing liquid over the surface of one side of the folder.

3. Allow the dishwashing liquid on the folder to dry.

4. Place the Epsom salts in a glass.

5. Add 3 tablespoons (45 ml) of warm water from the faucet to the glass containing the Epsom salts.

6. Stir until all of the salt dissolves in the water.

7. Place 3 tablespoons (45 ml) of Epsom salts solution on top of the dried

detergent on the folder. Use the bowl of the spoon to spread the solution as evenly as possible over the folder's surface.

8. Observe and record the changes that occur. If the air is dry and warm, the results take about 30 minutes. A longer time is required in cold and/or humid air.

9. Look through the folder toward a light. Notice and record the shape of the crystals.

RESULTS

Fans of long, clear, needle-shaped crystals form on the surface of the folder.

WHY?

As the water evaporates, the Epsom salts molecules move closer together and **bond** (link together), forming long, needle-shaped **crystals** (a solid material in which the molecules are arranged in a repeating pattern). The shape of the Epsom salts crystals reflects the arrangement of the molecules in the solid. The molecules are arranged like building blocks that lock together, and, thus, the shape of the molecules determines the resulting shape of the crystal. The dried dishwashing liquid provides a rough surface to which the crystals can stick.

LET'S EXPLORE

1. Will other crystals grow by evaporating the solvent (water) from the solution? Repeat the experiment using different solutes (the solid dissolved in the water) such as table salt, sugar, and alum. **Science Fair Hint:** Keep crystal samples for display along with a description of each crystal.

2. Would the speed of evaporation affect the shape of the resulting crystals? Repeat the experiment using Epsom salts. Prepare three different folders. Change the evaporation time by placing the folders in different places, such as in a refrigerator, in front of a fan, and at room temperature on a table. Observe the folders often, and record the time of the observation and the results.

SHOW TIME!

1. Another method of growing crystals by evaporation is to mix ½ cup (125 ml) of table salt with 1 cup (250 ml) of water in a drinking glass. Suspend a weighted cotton string into the salt solution, and observe for two to three weeks. Keep a journal to record the daily results. The journal and resulting crystal growth can be displayed.

2. Find out the different shapes that crystals can have, and make drawings to display. A visit to a rock-and-mineral shop will provide an opportunity to purchase inexpensive samples that can be used to represent the different crystal shapes. These samples can be displayed as part of a project, but your most impressive samples will be the crystals you grow yourself.

CHECK IT OUT!

How does gravity affect the growth of crystals? Why do crystals grown in space have a more perfect shape, and why is this important? Your parent or teacher can assist you in writing to NASA for information.

13

HONEYCOMBS

PROBLEM

Does salt affect the grouping of water molecules into ice crystals?

MATERIALS

masking tape
marking pen
2 small bowls
1-cup (250 ml) measuring
 cup
distilled water
1 teaspoon (5 ml) salt
spoon
freezer

PROCEDURE

1. Use the tape and marking pen to label the bowls #1 and #2.

2. Fill the measuring cup one-fourth full (60 ml) with distilled water.

3. Add the salt to the water in the cup. Stir.

4. Measure 2 tablespoons (30 ml) of salty water from the measuring cup into bowl #1.

5. Measure 2 tablespoons (30 ml) of distilled water into bowl #2.

6. Place both bowls in a freezer.

7. Observe and record any changes in the water in each bowl every five minutes until ice crystals are observed in one of the bowls. (Open the freezer each time for as short a period as possible.)

8. Leave the bowls in the freezer for 24 hours. Observe the liquids in each bowl every five minutes for one hour and again after 24 hours. Record the results.

RESULTS

Ice crystals form in bowl #2 containing the distilled water in about 10 to 20 minutes. Even after 24 hours, bowl #1 containing the salt water has no ice crystals.

WHY?

The symbol for a water molecule is H_2O. This indicates that one molecule of water is made of two hydrogen atoms (H) bonded to one oxygen (O) atom. The side of the molecule with the oxygen atom is negative and the side with the hydrogen atoms is positive. Because water molecules are electrically charged, they attract charged particles, including other water molecules.

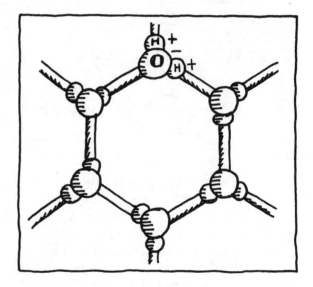

As the temperature of the water decreases, the molecules move closer together and link to form a six-sided honeycomb structure called ice.

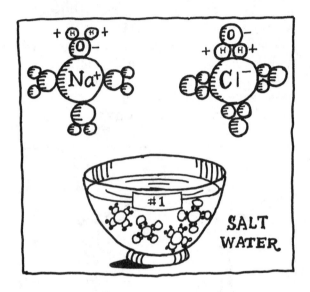

SALT WATER

When salt (NaCl) dissolves in water, each molecule breaks into two charged parts, sodium (Na^+) and chlorine (Cl^-). Atoms such as Na^+ and Cl^- that have charges (indicated by the plus and minus signs) are called **ions.** The sodium and chlorine ions are attracted to the charged water molecule. Salty water has water molecules bonded to the separate sodium

and chlorine ions instead of to other water molecules. Without the honeycomb structure, there are no ice crystals.

LET'S EXPLORE

1. Would a lesser amount of salt allow some of the water molecules to form ice crystals? Use different amounts of salt and record the results.

2. Would other **solutes** (substances that dissolve in the water) affect the freezing of water? Repeat the experiment using sugar and/or other materials that dissolve in water. Record the amount of each solute used and the results.

3. Which freezes faster, warm water or cold water? Place 1 tablespoon (15 ml) of cold water in a cup and 1 tablespoon (15 ml) of warm water in another cup. Set the cups in a freezer, and check every five minutes until ice crystals are seen in one of the cups. Repeat the experiment several times before making a conclusion. **Science Fair Hint:** You may want to place a thermometer in each cup. The temperature changes can give you more information to use when presenting your conclusion about this problem.

SHOW TIME!

1. Ice crystals do not form from only liquid water. Frost forms when water vapor (gas) changes directly to a solid. To demonstrate how frost forms, place a drinking glass in a freezer for 30 minutes. Remove the glass and allow it to stand undisturbed for one minute. A cloudy-looking layer of frost will form on the outside of the glass. Photographs of the glass before and after being placed in the freezer can be displayed.

2. Hailstones contain layers of ice. These stones form when snowflakes melt and then freeze again as they are moved up and down in a cloud by strong winds. Droplets of water freeze onto the moving stones, forming layers as the stones grow in size. Find out why hailstones most often form during warm weather. Display a diagram showing the growth of a hailstone as it moves up and down in a cloud.

CHECK IT OUT!

Why do ice molecules take up more space than an equal number of liquid water molecules? Find out why the chilled water molecules expand (move farther apart) when forming ice crystals.

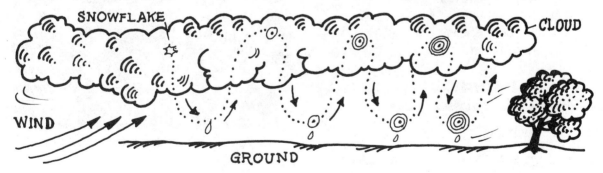

55

COLOR CHANGES

14

PROBLEM

Can stretching or twisting molecules in a solid cause a color change?

MATERIALS

two pairs of polarized
  sunglasses *Note: It is
  important that they are
  labeled "polarized."*
helper
1 foot (30 cm) clear
  aquarium tubing

PROCEDURE

1. Put one pair of glasses on.

2. Face a window.

3. Hold the second pair of glasses as far from your face as your outstretched arms will allow.

4. Have a helper hold the aquarium tubing near, but not touching, the glasses in your hand. The tubing should be between you and the glasses.

5. Look at the tubing through your polarized glasses while your helper holds the tubing.

6. Continue to look at the tubing through your polarized glasses while your helper pulls on the tubing to make it a tight line.

7. While the tubing is stretched tight, ask your helper to rotate the ends of the tubing in opposite directions.

RESULTS

The tube appears colorless before it is stretched. It takes on many different colors when pulled and rotated. If it does not, your lenses are not polarized. To check the glasses for polarization, put on one pair and hold the second pair in front of your eyes. Slowly rotate the pair of glasses you are holding. If the lenses are polarized, when you have turned the second pair of glasses a certain amount, nearly all light will be blocked out.

WHY?

Sunlight contains seven different colors: red, orange, yellow, green, blue, indigo, and violet. The color of an object depends on the color of light it reflects. If it reflects all colors, it is seen as white. An object that does not reflect any light will look black. Objects have color because of molecules. The shape of the molecules in the object causes some of the colors from light to be absorbed and some to be reflected. A green apple looks green because it contains molecules that reflect green light. As the apple ripens, the shape of the molecules in the apple change, and their new structure reflects red light; thus, the apple looks red. The molecular change in the apple is due to a chemical change, but molecular changes can be caused by stretching and rotating the object. The molecules in the aquarium tubing move around and change shape as the tube is stretched and rotated. With each structure change, the color of reflected light changes, and, thus, the color of the tube changes.

Note: For information about why the lenses are called polarized and how they work, see an experiment called "A Rainbow of Colors" on page 68, *Teaching the Fun of Physics* by Janice VanCleave (New York: Prentice-Hall, Inc., 1987).

LET'S EXPLORE

1. How would a different number of polarized lenses affect the results? Repeat the experiment first using one polarized lens and then using three polarized lenses.

2. Is it necessary to have only polarized lenses? Repeat the experiment replacing one pair of sunglasses with a pair of glasses with nonpolarized lenses.

SHOW TIME!

1. Would molecules in a liquid change colors if stretched? Soap bubbles provide one way to demonstrate color changes in liquids. Use a commercially prepared soap-bubble solution to blow bubbles. Observe the surface of the bubbles and record the colors observed as the bubble changes due to the force of gases inside

and the force of gravity pulling down on the thin film. Display colored drawings of the bubbles.

2. In clear materials, does the thickness of the material (layers of molecules) cause color changes? Drop clear fingernail polish into a bowl of water. Place the bowl away from direct light and observe the surface of the water from different angles. A rainbow of colors will be seen in the thin layers of the fingernail polish. Try other transparent (see-through) liquids, such as oil. Make diagrams to use as part of a

project display. With luck, a photograph might capture the colors on the water's surface. Use the photograph to represent the experiment even if the colors are not visible.

3. Observe and record examples of common color changes. Use photographs and/or diagrams to display examples such as:
- the color of ocean water as the depth changes
- egg whites before and after beating
- stretching a balloon

CHECK IT OUT!

The earth is called the "blue planet" because of the blue color of its atmosphere. Find out how the molecules in the atmosphere affect the sun's light and, thus, make the sky look blue from the earth and give the entire planet a blue look when it is observed from space. An experiment called "Blue Sky" on page 28 in *Astronomy for Every Kid,* (New York: Wiley, 1991), by Janice VanCleave can be used as a source of information.

I.D.

15

PROBLEM

How do dissolved materials change water molecules to form an acidic or basic solution?

MATERIALS

2 1-quart (1 liter) jars, one with a lid
distilled water
red cabbage
1-cup (250 ml) measuring cup
wooden spoon
wire tea strainer
masking tape
marking pen
5 8-oz (250 ml) clear plastic drinking glasses
2 teaspoons (10 ml) baking soda
2 teaspoons (10 ml) cream of tartar

PROCEDURE

1. Fill the jar that has a lid half full with distilled water.

2. Tear red cabbage leaves into small pieces. Add 2 cups (500 ml) of the cabbage leaves to the jar of water.

3. Press against the leaves in the jar with the wooden spoon so that the leaves are crushed, allowing some of the cabbage juice to escape.

4. Close the lid on the jar, and vigorously shake until the water in the jar takes on a pale purple color.

5. Pour the pale purple liquid through the wire strainer and into the empty jar.

6. Use the masking tape and marking pen to label the jar "INDICATOR."

7. Fill one plastic glass one-fourth full with distilled water, and add the baking soda. Stir.

8. Label the glass "BASE."

9. Fill a second plastic glass one-fourth full with distilled water, and add the cream of tartar. Stir.

10. Label this glass "ACID."

11. Into each of three plastic glasses, pour ¼ cup (60 ml) of INDICATOR.

12. Label these glasses #1, #2, and #3.

13. Pour ACID into glass #2 to half fill the glass.

14. Pour BASE into glass #3 to half fill the glass.

15. Observe and record the colors in glass #1, glass #2, and glass #3.

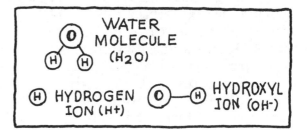

WATER MOLECULE (H₂O)

HYDROGEN ION (H+)

HYDROXYL ION (OH−)

RESULTS

Red Cabbage Indicator		
Indicator	Indicator + Acid	Indicator + Base
Glass #1	Glass #2	Glass #3
Pale Purple	Pink	Blue-Green

WHY?

Water is able to dissolve most substances with which it comes in contact, and these materials influence the acidic or basic properties of the water. Each water molecule is made of two hydrogen atoms and one oxygen atom (H_2O). Dissolved materials can cause the water molecule to produce charged particles called **ions.** If free hydrogen ions (H^+) are produced, the water becomes acidic. If hydroxyl ions (OH^-) are produced, the water becomes basic. Substances like baking soda that produce hydroxyl ions when dissolved in water are called bases, and substances like cream of tartar that produce hydrogen ions when dissolved in water are called acids. The red cabbage is called an indicator because it indicates the presence of hydroxyl ions by changing from its normal pale purple color to blue-green. The cabbage juice indicates the presence of hydrogen ions by changing from pale purple to pink. The shape of the molecules in the juice causes purple light to be reflected, causing the liquid to look purple. The presence of hydrogen ions or hydroxyl ions changes the shape of the molecules in the juice; the light reflected by the molecules is changed; the color of the juice changes.

SHOW TIME!

1. Do all materials that dissolve in water produce hydrogen or hydroxyl ions? Prepare and test the following materials using red cabbage indicator: salt, sugar, flour, cleaning powder, Epsom salts, vinegar, lemon juice. Prepare the solids by adding 2 teaspoons (10 ml) of each solid material to 1 cup (250 ml) of distilled water. The liquid materials can be added directly to the indicator solution. No change in color indicates a **neutral solution,** one that is neither acidic nor basic. A chart of the resulting colors along with conclusions of each test can be used as part of a project display.

2. Can other dyes extracted from plants be used as indicators? Test with juices from grapes, blackberries, or other berries. Use a solution of 1 teaspoon (5 ml) of turmeric (a spice) to 1 cup (250 ml) of rubbing alcohol. (*Note: Do not allow alcohol to get near mouth or eyes.*) Try other colored spices. Display examples of the different indicators used and their results. Some of the extracts will indicate the presence of an acid or of a base, but not both. In your

conclusion, point out the best indicator for testing for acids and bases.

3. Find out more about acids and bases. What are some common examples of acids and bases? Prepare a display of foods representing acids and bases by using photos cut out of magazines.

CHECK IT OUT!

Acid indigestion is due to an excessive production of stomach acid. Find out what acid is produced in the stomach and what causes an excess production of the acid. How do antacid tablets remove the excess stomach acid? A physician or pharmacist can provide information about this.

16

STRETCHY

PROBLEM

How does heat affect the movement of molecules in a rubber band?

MATERIALS

pencil
1 5-ounce (150 ml) paper cup
scissors
ruler
string
rubber band about 3 inches
   (7.5 cm) long
salt
table
masking tape
hair drier *(Note: Use only
   with adult supervision.)*

PROCEDURE

1. Use a pencil to punch two holes under the rim of the paper cup on opposite sides.

2. Cut an 8-inch (20 cm) length of string.

3. Tie the ends of the string through each hole in the cup to form a loop.

4. Cut the rubber band once to make one long 6-inch (15 cm) strip.

5. Tie one end of the rubber band to the string loop on the cup.

6. Cut an 18-inch (45 cm) length of string, and attach it to the free end of the rubber band.

7. Fill the cup about half full with salt.

8. Set the cup on the floor under the edge of a table.

9. Place the free end of the string on a table.

10. Slowly pull the string across the table. When the cup is just resting on the floor, tape the string to the top of the table.

STRING

RUBBER
BAND

STRING

11. Ask an adult to hold the hair drier turned to high heat about 2 inches (5 cm) from the rubber band and move it up and down the band.

12. Observe the position of the cup as the rubber band is heated for about ten seconds.

13. Remove the heat, and observe the cup for about 20 seconds.

RESULTS
The cup rises slightly off the floor when the rubber band is heated and returns to its original position as the rubber cools.

WHY?
Heating the rubber band causes the rubber molecules to vibrate (move around). The moving molecules separate slightly and slip past each other, causing the band to thicken and become shorter.

LET'S EXPLORE

1. Does the size of the rubber band change the movement of the heated band? Repeat the experiment using bands of various thicknesses. Place a yardstick (meterstick) beside the hanging cup to measure any difference in the movement of the cup.

HEAT COOL

RETURNED TO ORIGINAL POSITION

Science Fair Hint: Display the rubber bands used and the results when heated.

2. Does the weight of the cup affect the movement of the heated rubber band? Repeat the experiment using measured amounts of salt in the cup. Record the amounts of salt and the measured distance the cup moved when the rubber band was heated.

Do all solid materials contract (shrink) when heated? Replace the rubber band with a 22-gauge wire the same length as the rubber band. (Ask an adult to remove any insulation from the wire.) Try using other solid materials. The results from this experiment will indicate that the contraction of the rubber band when heated is contrary to the reaction of most heated materials. Heating generally causes molecules to spread apart, and, thus, the object expands. Include this information in your report, and use photographs of each of the experiments as part of the project display.

CHECK IT OUT!

1. Why do you think bridges, roads, and sidewalks are made with cracks?

2. Why does heating the metal lid on a jar with warm water make the lid easier to remove?

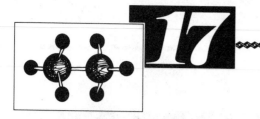

HEAVY WATER

17

PROBLEM

How does temperature affect the movement of water molecules?

MATERIALS

1-quart (1 liter) jar
ice cubes
water
2 coffee cups
green food coloring
2 clear drinking glasses
2 long-stemmed funnels
eyedropper

PROCEDURE

1. Fill the jar half full with ice. Then add water to cover the ice. Allow to stand for two minutes.

2. Fill one of the cups one-fourth full with the cold water from the jar. Add 10 drops of food coloring to the cold water.

3. Fill one of the glasses three-fourths full with warm water from the faucet.

4. Stand the funnel in the glass of warm water.

5. Fill the eyedropper with the cold colored water from the cup.

6. Hold the eyedropper above the funnel. Into the funnel, release drops of colored water one at a time until the color is observed coming out of the end of the funnel's stem.

7. Observe and record the movement of the colored water after it leaves the stem of the funnel.

8. Fill the second glass three-fourths full with cold water from the jar.

11. Fill the eyedropper with the warm colored water from the cup.

12. Hold the eyedropper above the funnel. Into the funnel, release drops of colored water one at a time until the color is observed coming out of the end of the funnel's stem.

13. Observe and record the movement of the colored water after it leaves the stem of the funnel.

9. Fill the second cup one-fourth full with warm water from the faucet. Add 10 drops of food coloring to the warm water.

10. Stand the funnel in the glass of cold water.

RESULTS

Streams of warm colored water rise in the cold water, and the cold colored water sinks in the warm water, forming a layer in the bottom of the glass.

WHY?

Cold water is heavier than warm water because the cold water molecules contract (get closer together) and the warm water molecules expand (get farther apart). This causes a drop of cold water to have more water molecules than a drop of warm water has. The **density** (the mass of a specific volume) of a drop of cold water is greater than the density of a drop of warm water. The denser cold water sinks and the less dense warm water rises. This up-and-down movement of the water molecules is called a **convection current**.

LET'S EXPLORE

1. Would it matter where the colored water was released? Repeat the experiment omitting the funnel and using the

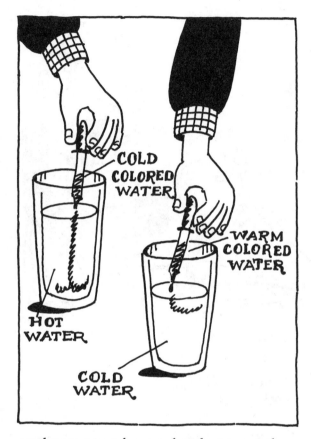

eyedropper to release colored water at the surface of the liquid in the glass. **Science Fair Hint:** Use diagrams similar to those shown to represent the procedure and results of this experiment. A description of the results along with the diagrams can be used as part of a project display.

2. Do convection currents occur in other liquids? Repeat the experiment using dishwashing liquid in place of water. Use dishwashing liquid at room temperature and some that has been chilled in the freezer.

SHOW TIME!

1. Do convection currents take place in gases as well as in liquids? Measure the temperature of the air in a room at the floor and ceiling levels. Do this by placing one thermometer on the floor and one as close as possible to the ceiling. Read and record the temperature every hour from morning until night. Prepare a chart showing the times of the readings and the temperatures. Use a diagram showing the positions of the thermometers, the data chart, and a conclusion of the results as part of a project display.

2. Find and display examples of convection currents in gases and liquids

such as:
- smoke rising in a chimney
- water heated in a water heater
- winds
- currents in the sea

CHECK IT OUT!

Find out how the differences in the density of materials in the earth's mantle produce convection currents. How do these currents affect the positions of continents?

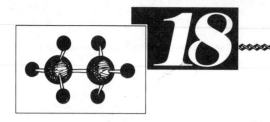

CLEANSING POWER

PROBLEM

How does dishwashing liquid clean away oil?

MATERIALS

4 clear drinking glasses
distilled water
masking tape
marking pen
4 1-teaspoon (5 ml)
   measuring spoons
cooking oil
dishwashing liquid

PROCEDURE

1. Fill each glass half full with distilled water.

2. Use the masking tape and marking pen to number the glasses #1 through #4.

3. Using a different measuring spoon each time, add 1 teaspoon (5 ml) of cooking oil to glass #2 and glass #4, and add 1 teaspoon (5 ml) of dishwashing liquid to glass #3, placing the spoons in the glasses after measuring.

4. Then add 1 teaspoon (5 ml) of the dishwashing liquid to the water and oil in glass #4.

5. Place a clean spoon in glass #1.

6. Stir the contents of each glass 25 turns.

7. Observe and record the appearance of the contents of each glass immediately after stirring.

8. Allow the glasses to stand undisturbed for five minutes.

9. Again observe and record the appearance of the contents of each glass.

RESULTS

Glass	Contents after Stirring	Contents after Standing 5 Minutes
#1	clear	clear
#2	drops of oil swirling throughout the water	circles of oil floating on the water's surface
#3	clear with some foam	clear
#4	cloudy with tiny bubbles floating in water, some foam	cloudy liquid

WHY?

Glasses #3 and #4 contain detergent from the dishwashing liquid. Detergent molecules are long and have one end that attracts water and another end that attracts oil. Stirring the liquid breaks the oil into tiny droplets. Detergent molecules surround and attach to each droplet of oil. The outside of the detergent molecule attaches to water drops. The oil remains in tiny drops suspended throughout the glass of water but separated from the water by a protective coat of detergent molecules. This allows oily dirt to be removed from dishes and dissolved in the dishwater containing detergent.

DETERGENT MOLECULE

LET'S EXPLORE

Would the amount of dishwashing liquid affect the results? Repeat the experiment using different amounts of dishwashing liquid.

SHOW TIME!

1. Is there a difference in the effectiveness of different brands of dishwashing liquids? Repeat the experiment using different brands. Take photographs or find advertising pictures of the different products used. Display these pictures with the "results" chart and the final summary report comparing the effectiveness of the product.

2. Do shampoos contain detergent? Repeat the experiment replacing the dishwashing liquid with a liquid shampoo. Since the ingredients of shampoos are often kept secret from competitors and consumers, you can only conclude that the cleanser contains a chemical that behaves like a detergent in its ability to disperse oils and grease. Make a comparison of the effectiveness of shampoos, and display the results along with a conclusion about the best shampoo as indicated by your testings.

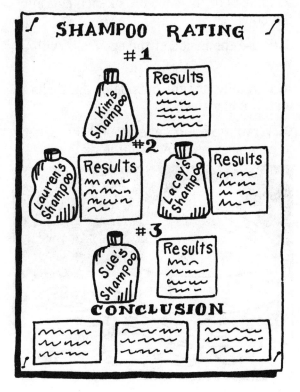

CHECK IT OUT!

1. Detergent molecules are said to have a split personality because of the different behaviors of each end of the molecule. Find out why one end of the molecule is called **hydrophilic** and the rest of the molecule is **hydrophobic.**

2. How are protein stains, such as grass, eggs, and blood, removed from clothing? What are enzymes, and how are the long chains of connected protein molecules wrapped around the tiny fibers in cloth cut into pieces by enzyme cleaners? What is the source of these dirt-snipping enzymes?

SUPPORTERS

How does the molecular structure of an eggshell affect its strength?

MATERIALS

metal spoon
4 raw eggs in their shells
bowl
water
paper towels
masking tape
nail scissors
books
bathroom scale

PROCEDURE

1. Using the edge of a spoon, carefully break off the small end of each eggshell. If any cracks form up the side of a shell, discard it and use another egg.

2. Shake out the contents of each egg into the bowl.

3. Rinse the inside of the eggshells with water.

4. Carefully dry the outside of the shells with a paper towel.

5. Wrap a piece of tape around the center of each shell as shown on the diagram.

The position of the tape should be the same on each shell.

6. Use nail scissors to cut away the broken ends of the shell from around the bottom of the tape on each shell.

7. Place the shells, open end down, in a rectangular array on a table.

8. Place a book on top of the shells, and position the shells so one is under each corner of the book.

9. Carefully add books, one at a time, to the book on top of the eggshells, waiting 30 seconds before adding each book. Keep adding books until a cracking sound is heard.

10. Record the number of books required to produce the crack.

11. Continue to carefully stack the books until the shells collapse.

12. Use a bathroom scale to weigh the books required to crack the shells and then the total weight that crushed the shells.

RESULTS

The number of books the eggs will hold depends on the weight of each book and the shape of the eggs used. [The author's result was that five books totaling 15 pounds (6.8 kg) produced the first crack, and two additional smaller books, bringing the total weight to 19 pounds (8.6 kg), crushed the eggs.]

WHY?

The eggshells are made of calcium carbonate molecules. The molecules are bonded together to form the solid structure around the content of the egg. The dome shape formed by the molecules provides a structure imitated by architects because of its strength and ability to span a large area. The weight placed on top of each egg is spread down along the curved sides to the base. No single point on the dome supports the whole weight, so together they can support quite a heavy weight.

LET'S EXPLORE

Would the eggshells support more or less weight if the small end of the shell was used? Repeat the experiment, but break off the large end of the shell. Record the number and weight of books that caused the first crack and then the number and weight needed to crush the shells. **Science Fair Hint:** As part of a project display, prepare new shells from the large and

Rounded Domes Supported ____ lbs. (__ Kg)

Pointed Domes Supported ____ lbs. (__ Kg)

small ends of the eggs. Exhibit the shells supporting lightweight books. Label the display with the total amount of weight that each set of eggs can support.

SHOW TIME!

1. How are molecules arranged in solids? Molecules in solids are not packed tightly together; much space exists in a solid. Explain and diagram how the "holding forces" among the molecules in a solid give it a definite shape and a definite volume and affect its strength.

2. Observe and collect samples of different types of solids. Make comparisons and draw conclusions about the strength of each type of material. Make a list of questions about the samples collected such as these and discover the answers: Are all wooden pieces hard? Can all samples of cloth be easily torn, and does the cloth tear with the same ease in all directions? Do all paper samples have the same strength? Display the samples, a list of your questions, and the answers to each question.

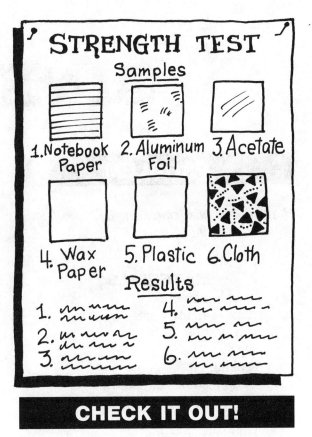

CHECK IT OUT!

Weight can be successfully hung from some solids but not others. This is due to the tensile strength of the material. What is **tensile strength?** Which solids have great tensile strength?

SINKERS

PROBLEM

How do molecules cause one liquid to float on another liquid?

MATERIALS

masking tape
clear drinking glass
marking pen
ruler
cooking oil
1-cup (250 ml) measuring
   cup
water
light corn syrup

PROCEDURE

1. Place a piece of tape down the side of the glass.

2. Using a ruler and marking pen, mark three lines on the tape at these distances from the bottom of the glass: 1 inch (2.5 cm), 2 inches (5 cm), and 3 inches (7.5 cm).

3. Pour cooking oil into the glass up to the 1-inch (2.5 cm) mark on the tape.

4. Fill the measuring cup with water and slowly pour the water down the inside wall of the glass containing the oil until the liquid level is at the 2-inch (5 cm) mark.

5. Observe the positions of the water and oil in the glass.

6. Pour enough light corn syrup into the glass to bring the top surface of the liquid level with the 3-inch (7.5 cm) mark.

7. Observe the position of all three liquids in the glass.

density of the liquids depends on the size and number of molecules in a certain volume. Some things float and others sink in water. Materials that float on water have a lesser density than water. Oil is less dense than water; this means that the molecules of oil weigh less than the same volume of water molecules. The density of the syrup is greater than the density of water or oil, so the syrup sinks in water and in oil and is thus the lowest layer. It is just as true to say that because the oil and water have a lesser density than syrup, they float above the syrup.

RESULTS

The three liquids form three separate layers with the syrup on the bottom, the water in the middle, and the oil floating on top.

WHY?

Density is the amount of weight that a material has for a specific volume. The

OIL
WATER
SYRUP

LET'S EXPLORE

1. Would the order in which the liquids are added to the glass affect the results?

Pour the liquids into the glass in a different order. Make an effort to pour each new liquid down the inside wall of the glass.

2. Will solids float on the surface of the different liquid layers? Add small pieces of solid one at a time and record the layer each solid floats on. Use things such as: toothpicks, match sticks, ice, tacks, paper clips, buttons, and beads. **Science Fair Hint:** A diagram showing the position of the objects and liquids can be displayed with an explanation of why they sink or float.

SHOW TIME!

1. Why is it easy to float in the Great Salt Lake? Find the answer to this by placing a fresh egg in water and then in salt water. Vary the amount of salt in the water to discover if it makes a difference. Diagrams of the container and the position of the egg in fresh and salty water can be displayed along with a photograph or picture of a person floating in a lake labeled Great Salt Lake.

2. Can you decide which substances will sink or float without putting them in the liquid? Ask your librarian or science teacher to assist you in finding a density chart in the appendix of a chemistry book or in a handbook of chemistry and physics. Use the chart to make a diagram showing the positions of liquids and solids with different densities.

CHECK IT OUT!

Find out how differences in the density of water can cause ocean currents. Find this information by reading about density and turbidity currents.

Acid A material that provides free hydrogen ions (H^+), tastes sour, neutralizes bases, and turns red cabbage juice pink.

Adhesion Force of attraction between unlike molecules.

Atom The smallest part of an element that shows the properties of the element; contains positive protons and neutral neutrons in its nucleus with negatively charged electrons spinning around the outside of the nucleus.

Attract To be pulled together.

Base Produces hydroxyl ions (OH^-), tastes bitter, neutralizes acids, and turns red cabbage juice blue.

Bond A connection between molecules.

Capillary Action The movement of water up through tiny tubes due to adhesive and cohesive forces.

Charged Having an excess of either negative or positive particles.

Coagulate To group together in a thickened mass; to change from a liquid to a solid form.

Cohesion Force of attraction between like molecules.

Concentrated Contains large quantities of solute dissolved in a solvent.

Contract To move closer together; to get smaller in size. Molecules move closer when cooled.

Convection Currents The movement of gases or liquids such that heated gases or liquids rise and are replaced by a cooler, heavier gas or liquid.

Crystal A solid containing molecules arranged in an orderly, repeating, three-dimensional pattern.

Denaturing Changing the natural form of a substance.

Density The scientific way of comparing the "heaviness" of materials; the measurement of the mass of a specific volume.

Diffusion The mixing of molecules because of molecular motion; the movement of molecules from one place to another that results in an even distribution of the molecular particles.

Dilute To lessen the strength of a solution by adding more solvent.

Electron A negatively charged particle moving within an area around the outside of the nucleus of an atom.

Electron Shell All of the paths of an electron; found outside the nucleus of an atom.

Ethane A hydrocarbon containing two carbon and six hydrogen atoms.

Expand To get larger; to take up more space. Molecules move apart and take up more space when heated.

Freeze To change a liquid to a solid by reducing the heat content of the liquid.

Homogeneous The same throughout.

Hydrocarbon Molecules composed of carbon and hydrogen atoms.

Immiscible The inability of two liquids to mix.

Indicator Chemical used to test for the presence of an acid or base; red cabbage.

Ion An atom that has a positive or negative charge.

Matter The substance things are made of. Matter takes up space and has weight.

Meringue Whipped egg whites.

Methane Simplest hydrocarbon; contains one carbon and four hydrogen atoms.

Model A simple way of describing an idea; can be a picture, word description, or three-dimensional structure.

Molecule The smallest part of a substance that keeps the properties of the substance; tiny parts that make up matter. The linking of two or more atoms produces a molecule.

Neutron A positively charged particle found within the nucleus of an atom.

Osmosis The movement of a material such as water through a membrane from an area of greater amounts of water to an area of lesser amounts of water.

Proton A positively charged particle found (already charged) within the nucleus of an atom.

Reflect To bounce back from a surface.

Saturated Solution A solution in which, at a constant temperature, a solvent contains the maximum amount of dissolved solute.

Solute The substance that breaks into smaller parts and moves throughout a solvent. In a sugar-and-water mixture, sugar would be the solute.

Solution The combination of a solute with a solvent. Sugar plus water produces a solution.

Solvent The substance that a solute dissolves in. In a sugar-and-water mixture, water would be the solvent.

Surface Tension The tendency of liquid molecules to cling together at the surface to form a skinlike film across the surface of the liquid.

Vibrate The quick back-and-forth movement of molecules in a small space.

Wetting The ability of water to cover a surface; requires adhesion between the molecules in the water and the molecules in the surface material.

INDEX

**Get these fun and exciting books by Janice VanCleave
at your local bookstore, call toll-free 1-800-225-5945
or visit our Web site at: www.wiley.com/children/**

Janice VanCleave's Science for Every Kid Series

____Astronomy	53573-7	$11.95 US / 15.95 CAN
____Biology	50381-9	$11.95 US / 15.95 CAN
____Chemistry	62085-8	$11.95 US / 15.95 CAN
____Constellations	15979-4	$11.95 US / 15.95 CAN
____Dinosaurs	30812-9	$10.95 US / 15.95 CAN
____Earth Science	53010-7	$11.95 US / 15.95 CAN
____Ecology	10086-2	$10.95 US / 15.95 CAN
____Geography	59842-9	$11.95 US / 15.95 CAN
____Geometry	31141-3	$11.95 US / 15.95 CAN
____Human Body	02408-2	$11.95 US / 15.95 CAN
____Math	54265-2	$11.95 US / 15.95 CAN
____Oceans	12453-2	$12.95 US / 15.95 CAN
____Physics	52505-7	$11.95 US / 15.95 CAN

Janice VanCleave's Spectacular Science Projects Series

____Animals	55052-3	$10.95 US / 12.95 CAN
____Earthquakes	57107-5	$10.95 US / 12.95 CAN
____Electricity	31010-7	$10.95 US / 12.95 CAN
____Gravity	55050-7	$10.95 US / 12.95 CAN
____Insects & Spiders	16396-1	$10.95 US / 15.50 CAN
____Machines	57108-3	$10.95 US / 12.95 CAN
____Magnets	57106-7	$10.95 US / 12.95 CAN
____Microscopes & Magnifying Lenses	58956-X	$10.95 US / 12.95 CAN
____Molecules	55054-X	$10.95 US / 12.95 CAN
____Plants	14687-0	$10.95 US / 12.95 CAN
____Rocks & Minerals	10269-5	$10.95 US / 12.95 CAN
____Volcanoes	30811-0	$10.95 US / 12.95 CAN
____Weather	03231-X	$10.95 US / 12.95 CAN

Janice VanCleave's Science Bonanzas Series

____200 Gooey, Slippery, Slimy, Weird & Fun Experiments

57921-1 $12.95 US / 16.95 CAN

____201 Awesome, Magical, Bizarre & Incredible Experiments

31011-5 $12.95 US / 16.95 CAN

____202 Oozing, Bubbling, Dripping & Bouncing Experiments

14025-2 $12.95 US / 16.95 CAN

Janice VanCleave's Guide to the Best Science Fair Projects

____Guide to the Best Science Fair Projects

14802-4 $14.95 US / 19.95 CAN

Prices subject to change without notice.